Writing For All
The Wrong Reasons

Writing For All The Wrong Reasons

Liat Silver

Full Court Press
Englewood Cliffs, New Jersey

First Edition

Copyright © 2020 by Liat Silver

All rights reserved. No part of this book may be reproduced or transmitted in any form or by any means electronic or mechanical, including by photocopying, by recording, or by any information storage and retrieval system, without the express permission of the author, except where permitted by law.

Published in the United States of America by Full Court Press, 601 Palisade Avenue, Englewood Cliffs, NJ 07632
fullcourtpress.com

ISBN 978-1-946989-73-4
Library of Congress Catalog No. 2020913616

Editing and book design by Barry Sheinkopf

Cover art by Esther Brodsky

To my parents

*who taught me how loud my voice could be,
first through listening, then through saying these are words
everyone should hear.
They taught me how to speak and focus
on the thoughts that mattered.
So when the time would come for me to be heard
I wouldn't need a microphone, only the courage to share.*

Table of Contents

Introduction, 1

Emptiness, *3*
Sleepless Night, *15*
Rain / Cleanse, *25*
Thoughts, *37*
Lost, *57*
Saying Goodbye, *77*

WRITING FOR ALL THE WRONG REASONS

I have broken down many times before
and every time I built myself back up,
I pushed away the pieces
I no longer wanted to be part of me.
I re-created myself
time and time again,
and grew whole
with every piece I threw away.
I wanted to be better,
to rid myself of my imperfections
unknown to me
they lingered in all the words I wrote,
the emptiness I felt
the sleepless nights I suffered
the cleanse that followed rain
the thoughts that I erased
the worry of being lost —
they all ended up here.
This book is made of only imperfections,
the chapters of my life I wish to close.

Emptiness

WRITING FOR ALL THE WRONG REASONS

I felt empty,
I wrote poem after poem about it
and crumpled all the pages
in the hope that I could use the paper
to fill the hole.
The pages scratched me
their edges cutting me from the inside
my words too potent to allow me to survive.
The ink poisoned me
transformed my blood from red to black
and dyed my skin a dark shade of blue.
All of my attempts left me empty
possibly even more than I was to begin with
but I kept on writing in hope
that I could fix myself
until the moment I myself
became the poetry.

Last night I felt as though something inside me broke.
For the past few days I've been running on empty
and it's left a gap in my chest.
As hard as I have tried
no matter what I did,
I couldn't make myself feel whole again,
so I used glass to fill the empty space
and was left with a window revealing my soul.
I am now an open book,
an image painted with instructions.
I can no longer hide the destruction inside me,
it is forever on display.
Most nights I lie awake,
my eyes so heavy,
and my heart beats hard enough
to shatter the glass,
but I'm not fortunate enough to sleep,
my mind is too full of thoughts that come and go
like people on the street.
There are warning signs,
detours, streetlights and paths outlined in white.
I wish I knew why I never followed them.
Last night a piece of myself broke

and was replaced with thin glass,
leaving my secrets to show
and my heart on display.
I am a living ghost
held together by pieces that are not mine.
Such a sad story to tell,
such a fragile little creature.

I thought I could handle it
thought I was strong enough to stand on my own
but with every person I pushed away
in the interest of self-preservation
I rediscovered just how lonely it is
to have no one.
I felt alone even when I was with you.
Love is supposed to feel comforting,
Love I was told would make me feel whole,
yet I spent many nights thinking
about how the bed I slept in
had too much extra space
and even if you were lying there
right next to me
you felt a million miles away.
The people that I love
are not capable of staying.
Maybe that is why I am so afraid.
I know that they won't change their lives
to keep me in them,
so I must change everything
giving up so many of my dreams
so I do not lose anyone else.

WRITING FOR ALL THE WRONG REASONS

I am forced to cross oceans,
tightrope across mountaintops,
to stay with those who make me whole
even if the air of a new place
eats away at parts of me
I never worried about before.
The people I loved were never capable of staying,
so I forced myself to learn to be alone,
so when they finally left me not only
would I be able to survive
but I was prepared
because I knew the day would come.

I've come to realize
that I don't really miss you:
What I miss is having someone,
being loved
not being alone.
It was unforgettable
to see your picture and beyond feeling
nothing, feeling confused.
You were the boy I once imagined a future with,
the boy I was beginning to fall in love with.
But my feelings were stronger than my body,
and when you no longer loved
or even liked the little things about me,
those feelings slowly left,
removing an enormous weight
from my shoulders and my chest.
Some nights memories of ours appear
like a movie after I close my eyes.
I don't mean to think about you
truth be told, I don't want to
but for some reason
I torture myself night after night
by painting these images

onto the backs of my eyelids
almost as if allowing myself
to be at peace is wrong.
Your name no longer makes my heart jolt
my heart belongs more
to strangers on the street,
or boys who seem nice enough
to care about me,
more than it belongs to you.
In all my desperation just to feel
the comfort of having someone once again
I've accidentally fallen a little in love
with any boy who shows me
a bit of kindness
since it has been so long
since someone's been affectionate to me.
You made my ideals turn bitter
and ruined my chances of being with anyone
and not seeing you in them.
I don't miss you
But I so badly miss what we could have been.

My thoughts have been eating me alive
leading to the infamous hole in my chest.
I first tried to fill it with pills
hoping if I took enough
my emptiness would be transformed to something new.
When that didn't work,
I tried to fill it up with people,
unintentionally stealing their kindness,
using them as bricks to hide my vulnerability.
After the brick wall caved in
on itself I tried to fill my
gap with writing
swapping phony building blocks with poisonous ink
wondering if my written thoughts could feed the monster
my unspoken ones created.
Even that didn't work,
so I'm down to my last resort
finding the pieces that once made me whole
and one by one
gluing them back into my chest,
praying they still fit together after all this time
of me using random material to solve the puzzle
of the hollow girl and her self-destruction.

It scares me
something meant to help me and make me stronger,
a small white pill
has the power to destroy me,
and make me sick for days.
I'm missing parts of myself,
my brain chemistry so faulty
that doctors were forced to try to fix me,
but you cannot fix what isn't broken
so they mended me instead,
used pills and calming words
to bridge the gap between my mind
and my control
making me more secure for hours at a time
until construction stalls
and I crash from the highest ladder,
unable to pull myself together on my own
needing the help of little white pills
to function as a whole.

I was sick
I was an unbalanced mixture of chemistry and biology
and spent every day destroying myself from the inside out
until I learned how to cure what was wrong with me.
Now I fear that others will never understand me
if they know nothing of my illness
but I also fear how they might see me
once they know the truth.

Sleepless Night

WRITING FOR ALL THE WRONG REASONS

It's always at night
the loneliness and emptiness decide to join me
as I lie in a bed that feels too big for me
and acknowledge the space that no one's there to fill.
It's always at night
I'm reminded how hard it is to sleep
how many hours that I must spend alone
how long I have to stay completely still
and pray that my mind will pity me enough
to let me rest.
It's always at night
my anxieties sound so loud
a constant headache ringing in my ears
and silence that surrounds me
devours me
echoing all the voices in my head.
It's always at night
the self-pity and the heaviness in my chest begin to weigh me down.
They twist me in my blankets
and tuck me in so I am trapped
with nowhere to go.
It's always at night that words and poems
come to me

I hear their possibilities and sense relief
that they can bring me.
But lately I have only
been able to begin them and never end them,
they are my dreams before I even am asleep.
It's always in the morning
I wake up nervous
but optimistic for the day to come
filled with hope that today will be better
today I will be better
and tonight will be different.

Sleep no longer comes easy to me
but why should it?
how could my body rest
when my mind is running in circles?
— it's 2:00 a.m., and I can't sleep.

LIAT SILVER

After too many sleepless nights
filled with nightmares and tears,
and jolting awake covered in my sweat
I have decided that it is easier to give up sleep
then it is to close my eyes and welcome insanity
—it's 2:00 a.m. again and I don't want to sleep.

WRITING FOR ALL THE WRONG REASONS

You would think after all this time
I would run out of words to describe
my sleepless nights.
I've replaced my dreams with ink,
my pillows with crumpled-up pages,
and kept my sanity locked away in a journal,
but poetry is the only thing keeping the nightmares away
and I fear that once I stop
I'll never be able to fall asleep again
—sleep is for the brave.

LIAT SILVER

I am tired,
so tired I feel it in my bones
feel it weigh me down
causing me to use more energy than I possess
to perform the simplest functions.
Why then if I am so exhausted it debilitates me,
why can't I sleep?
How is it that my body lacks
a semblance of strength to carry on,
but my mind remains up and running
and scares away the sleep that creeps in at night?
This exhaustion that I feel cannot be natural.
Perhaps it is a side effect of all the time I've wasted
sleeping instead of living
the years of artificial energy,
hope and calm that lulled me to sleep
And now without them I can't do it on my own.
I forgot how to sleep similar to how I forgot
how to dream.
Sleep is cold and lifeless,
and my dreams are only dreams
in the form of nightmares,
so maybe

WRITING FOR ALL THE WRONG REASONS

just maybe
in trying to spare myself the horrors
that accompany sleep
I've forced myself into a constant state of exhaustion
in the hope that when I finally do sleep
I'll be too tired to dream.

My heart beats too quickly to remain in my chest—
it feels as if it is trying to escape,
my heart is afraid of something within me
and I have yet to discover what.
This poem has come to my mind before
but always remained in the back.
These words have repeated over and over again
as insistently as my heart beats
but I have pushed them away
in attempt to allow myself to sleep.
The beating of my heart has become my lullaby,
a lullaby too loud
too fast
and out of my control.
Every night in the quiet of my room
I hear it and beg it to calm down
so I may finally rest.
The beating of my heart
has kept me awake night after night,
almost as if I am afraid of sleeping.

WRITING FOR ALL THE WRONG REASONS

Rain / Cleanse

On rainy days my mind feels empty
allowing me a peace I otherwise would never know.
What does it say about me that I like rain?
What does it mean that I identify
not as the calm before the storm
but the calm during the storm,
the calm that can only belong to the storm.
I believe it means that my mind
is made up of storm clouds of its own.
On sunny days the clouds grow dark
and loom over me,
but on rainy days they are allowed freedom,
and my thoughts have the chance to move around
instead of haunting me while they hide in a corner in my mind.
But what does it mean for me
to love something so many people hate?
Have I made myself an outsider
in a place where safety is only found indoors?
Am I surrounded by those
who have no dark clouds of their own?
Perhaps this is the curse of a writer,
the ability to see the beauty in chaos
and understand there is meaning beyond the doors

meant to keep you dry.
Rain is too powerful to call an inconvenience,
it brings life and wipes away the bad,
creating a clean slate.
Rain is too powerful
to be considered anything but a miracle.
On rainy days my mind feels empty
my personal gray clouds now part
of one large cloud in the sky
and when they return they are no longer gray,
along with the thoughts they shape.

WRITING FOR ALL THE WRONG REASONS

You need a girl who will remind you that rain is good
that with every shower new life is brought to this world
that thunderstorms and lightning bolts
fix internal havoc
and the blankets that you're using to protect yourself
hold you so tight to keep you from falling apart.
You need a girl who will remind you
that even the stars have distances between them
that with every fallen star millions of wishes are made
that meteor showers and full moons are superstitions
meant to offer hope
and when night falls the stars that decorate the sky
watch over you to keep you safe.
You need a girl who will remind you it's all right to be scared
that fear can bring out the best in you
that the breath caught in your throat
and the extreme beating of your heart
are part of being human
and without it you would lose your sense of self.
You need a girl who will change your point of view
and show you beauty you have never seen before,
that windows are meant for gazing into your soul
that distance and longing bring people together in a way

LIAT SILVER

nothing else can
and the words you hide behind
reveal more than you mean to show.
You needed a girl
to be the moon to your stars
but you settled for a raindrop
before it ran down your window.

WRITING FOR ALL THE WRONG REASONS

I wonder
if I stand in the storm for long enough
could the rain replace the blood in my veins?
—I am a storm of my own.

How am I supposed to focus on a rainy day?
The thunder and pouring rain are too loud,
the lightning too bright,
the air too electric
to allow me to experience any other thoughts.

It was a rainy day,
the same as so many before it,
the thunder as loud as always
the lightning still striking so bright.
I had grown accustomed to days like this
to storms like this
yet I couldn't help but look out my window
and wonder if you still remember my fear of thunderstorms
if the worry was still as evident on your face
when the house shook from thunder
since you knew I was hiding under my blankets,
praying for the storm to pass,
it was something so insignificant
that meant the world to me
you would lift my blankets up
and hold me until the thunder stopped roaring,
you would promise that the storm couldn't hurt me
that I was safe as long as I was in your arms.
Storms don't scare me like they used to
the thunder never seems as loud as it used to be
my blankets no longer serve as protection from the storm
raging on
thunderstorms don't scare me the way they used to

instead they make me think
make me curious if the raindrops
that once created a halo around your head
had finally dried up
curious if you still remember my fear of thunderstorms
or have someone new to worry about.

The air is heavier on days like this.
The harder the rain pours,
the more challenging I find it to breathe
until I wonder if the world is now under water
and the rain I see is actually air trying to reach me.

Do you feel it in your bones as I do?
Feel the sunlight on your skin
and the wind drifting through your thoughts?
The making of a summer storm lives within me,
lightning and thunder threaten to tear me apart,
the rain promises to fill the voids created
but the sunlight,
the sunlight whispers to me that it is alright to be a storm
dangerous as it may be,
it's equally as beautiful.
Those who fear a summer storm
will never know peace
the sun will burn them,
the wind carry them away
their bones will ache unaware of what they're missing
and the rain will weigh them down
instead of healing them.
Be a storm,
powerful and balanced.
Welcome the storm:
Safety is found in those strange places.

Thoughts

WRITING FOR ALL THE WRONG REASONS

If all my feelings remain unjustified
it's because I sewed my heart onto my sleeve
and have been afraid to tear the stitching.

LIAT SILVER

With every person who comes and goes
I give and lose a piece of myself
while they remain whole.

My mother held me and whispered bravely enough to replace
the broken shards of myself I had lost along the way:
"You think you will never be truly over it,
never able to fully let go.
But I think it will hurt,
it will hurt so badly.
Until finally,
one day it won't hurt anymore."

LIAT SILVER

I have walked on many burning coals
and broken shards of glass
attempting to prove myself to people
who think so highly of themselves
that I could be six feet under
covered in dirt and blood and gasping for air
but still be told I have not done enough
to deserve their affection.

WRITING FOR ALL THE WRONG REASONS

Recently I have turned to writing
for all the wrong reasons,
hoping that if my poetry was strong enough,
I could win the world over.
My words no longer feel like mine,
they lack the safety that used to come
with being locked on paper;
they now feel as dangerous as the spoken word,
and I have grown as scared
to show my writing as I've been
to speak before a crowd.
What if I convey the wrong message?
What if my written word is ignored like my spoken one?
How do I tell the world who I am as a person
if I lack the confidence to talk?
I aspire for my words to be like a song,
to be stuck in your head all day
and make you to feel in ways you have not felt before,
to be read and listened to over and over again
until you can say it all from memory,
to be unforgettable and tug on your heart strings.
Instead I fear my pen in the bow;
my heart is the strings of the violin,
and I have played myself.

Falling apart but you don't seem to notice,
held together by duct tape, staple guns, and thorn bushes
filled with roses,
each and every day I have another excuse for why I'm broken
but none involve you.
I claim I'm my own being
so no one else will suffer the truth
I'm trying to piece myself together
but I'm incomplete without you.

I am broken
and that is a tough pill to swallow,
but in the interest of healing
I find myself taking one every morning and every night.
One day I will no longer need medicine to fix what is wrong with me
but until that day
I will continue to fill the gap in my chest
with synthetic happiness and safety.

As a writer I should not be fooled by words
I know the power they contain
but I also know how deceiving they can be.
Maybe it was wrong of me to doubt
the story you told me,
but I am a writer
and I feel too strongly
to change my narrative over false hope
—my feelings are not a toy.

WRITING FOR ALL THE WRONG REASONS

Maybe it's desperation,
throwing my feelings at the first boy
to look at me kindly
but it has been so long
since someone looked at me
instead of through me
that I'm willing to compromise my morality
for a chance to feel like the sun.

LIAT SILVER

The world has told us that we are made of glass
glass bodies with razor hands—
the gentlest of touch and we destroy each other,
the softest drop of rain and we shatter,
so in order to protect ourselves
we have put caution tape around our mouths,
and locked the doors that used to guide us to each other,
I fear for the day when we're all reunited,
perhaps by then all that will be left of humanity
is glass sculptures with metal engravings.

I thought if I threw out everything
that once belonged to you I would finally feel clean.
Instead I was left in an empty room
and the only part of me that still felt full
was the part that missed you.
This world used to be ours for the taking.
Maybe that is why everything now feels so tainted.
Why when I drag my fingertips over objects
that have not been touched since you left
my skin does not collect dust
but traces of you.

I thought it was love
comparing you to anything that brought me joy,
the smell of the rain,
the warmth of a hug,
the feel of fresh ink beneath my fingers.
But I have since learned that I know nothing of love,
I think that I accidentally convinced myself I loved you,
since I wrote so beautifully about you.

WRITING FOR ALL THE WRONG REASONS

I am weaker now than ever before,
a thought so terrifying
that perhaps I've used up all my strength
trying to fight it.

How do you write about love without having felt it?
Simple
you write about longing,
then change a few words.

Brittle bones
belonging to a girl made of glass
worn down by the weight of the world
and the words left unsaid.

LIAT SILVER

My thoughts planted a garden,
but words grew in place of flowers.

These words belong to me.
they are the remnants of the many lives I have lived
and the people I could not convince to stay.
These words that I have written
have become tattoos on my skin
telling a story
even to those who won't listen.

Lost

I like looking as if I belong somewhere.
My whole life has felt like a case of mistaken identity
almost as if I was one step away from being like everyone else
but that one step was so monumental
and required more strength than I possess.
I was a foreigner in my own country,
my own home.
I just could not belong.
There is no stranger feeling than fitting in
in a country with a foreign tongue
a place where I am not familiar
with the customs or the way of life.
I belong more in a place
where I simply do not know how to live
than I do where I was born and raised.
I fear it,
fear never truly and wholeheartedly belonging,
being an exotic creature in every land I visit.
My worlds are separated by oceans and plane rides,
and one day very soon
I must decide if I would rather live openly
as an outsider
or learn a new way of living
in a country as alien as I feel.

LIAT SILVER

I tried to keep myself from feeling certain things,
using everyday occurrences as distractions.
I drank coffee,
savoring its bitter taste
the way it made my body shake
since it was stronger than I was.
I took hot showers,
The water scalding and burned
turning my skin a raw shade of red,
washing away the memories I wanted to forget.
I walked through the day as if on barbed wire,
cutting my feet with every step I took
leaving bloody footprints that allowed me
to retrace my path,
teaching myself to be careful
and not wander off too far.
I did everything I could to control what I felt,
internalizing everything there was on the outside,
trying to force out what was naturally inside of me.

WRITING FOR ALL THE WRONG REASONS

Will you forget this place after you leave it?
Will it no longer be home once you've moved on to newer places?
Poets continue to write about home being a person not a place,
but if you are mine,
will I be left homeless?
I was born in a world not right for me,
my soul one in billions,
yet I feel so alone.
You were born in a place not right for you,
so you plan to move and leave it all behind
to leave me behind.
It's selfish of me to ask you to stay
but you are my home,
my safety and comfort,
you are what links me to a world I wish to leave behind.
But I am not enough to keep you where you don't belong.
I'm one in billions,
a shooting star on a cloudy night
I don't matter to many,
god knows I barely matter.
But I am your one in billions,
your shooting star,
and you are still going to leave me behind.
Please don't leave me behind.

LIAT SILVER

One day I am going to have to pack it all up
I will have to decide what's important enough to keep
and what I will have to throw away
or give to others
since they will not have a place in my new life
I worry more about the things I will leave behind
than those I will bring with me,
what will become of them?

WRITING FOR ALL THE WRONG REASONS

One year old,
this world is so very new
and there is so much you need to be protected from
sheltered from.
Oh, how you will grow.

Two years old,
you are growing bigger every day
the world is your playground
you are out to explore.
Please don't trip on the uneven ground.

Three years old,
you are a troublemaker
a bad habit that will take you years to outgrow,
but don't you fret
and please don't worry.
Everyone still loves you just the same
even if you are destructive.

Four years old,
living in a land of make-believe
sometimes it's hard to differentiate

between what's in your head
and what is real.
That is okay,
that is normal,
there is nothing wrong with you.

Five years old,
almost every story you tell ends with someone laughing.
Can they not tell that you were being serious?
You are a strange child,
and one day you'll grow up
to hear stories of all the things you did
and laugh loudly while silently wondering
why you did them.

Six years old,
you start to notice how different you are
from all the other girls,
you are not pretty in the same way they are,
you don't dress like they do,
you are an exotic creature who just wants to be
like everyone else.
Please learn to love your own skin.

Seven years old,
you have too much energy,

WRITING FOR ALL THE WRONG REASONS

your body is too small
for the soul it is meant to contain.
The desk before you and the chair beneath you
feel more like a prison than a throne,
all the simple things are too difficult
and some days you just want to give up.
Thank you for not giving up.

Eight years old,
another year of feeling misplaced:
You wish you could sit still and stay in place.
Almost everything you're told will be too much
for you to remember.
It's such a shame it all felt wasted on you.

Nine years old,
you begin to hear whispers of change,
suddenly a doctor's asking all these questions,
and you don't want to give the wrong answer.
there is nothing wrong with you,
there is something wrong with everyone else
but it is far easier to change one person
than the entire world.

Ten years old,
they tried to change you.

You can't control yourself on your own,
so somebody must do it for you.
You lost some of your shine this year,
the little white pills meant to help you hurt you
crushed you as you did them every morning,
Slowly you'll learn to breathe on your own again.

Eleven years old,
you are more tired than you like,
it feels as though all the things that made you you
have been locked away and held out of reach.
Some nights you lie awake and cannot sleep because your
stomach feels too empty and your mind too full,
this is a feeling you may never get used to.

Twelve years old,
you asked them to stop,
told them the little white pills were hurting
more than helping you,
but you were just a naive child—
how could you know what was best for you?

Thirteen years old,
you started growing up.
Your body changed and your view on the world was distorted.
You were afraid you would never find your place,

you still fear that to this day.
This was a hard year for you
the little things that feel so wrong
about you grow along with your small body.
You were meant to be a butterfly
but you feel more like an ant that's been crushed.

Fourteen years old,
you are sick,
more sick than anyone could ever have anticipated.
You are destroying yourself from the inside out.
Any attempt to save you has also lost you.
You are not you anymore.
You may not be anything.

Fifteen years old,
sixteen years old,
both years such a blur
you can only remember the bad,
truthfully you can't remember much.
It is so terrifying to forget yourself.

Seventeen years old,
you are so very scared of what comes next.
Seventeen feels far too young to start deciding your future.
In the year to come you will lose yourself and find someone new,

will you recognize her?
Is she really you?
You are older now, you may realize,
so why do you still feel like a child?

Eighteen years old,
you are your very own person.
Almost overnight you went from child to an adult,
you are more scared than hopeful
more lost than you ever thought possible.
You have given your heart away too many times
for it to remain whole.
Now you are an adult they will tell you,
but they will forget to teach you how.

The worst part of being an adult
is looking back at your childhood
and wishing you could stay there forever.
The worst part is still feeling
like a child but being told you're not one anymore.

My mouth has been sewn shut—
out of respect or fear, I cannot tell.
They told me never to talk back,
thinking it would keep me from harming others
or stepping over boundaries set by age.
But really it has only hurt me,
since I can't defend myself for fear of being disrespectful,
cannot stand my ground for fear of being too pushy.
After all these years,
even after the needle is no longer pressed to my lips
too often for me to remember how to speak,
I can't forget the pain I feel when I try to.
I am held back by invisible thread,
restrained by what I was taught was right
and what I learned was true.
My mouth was sewn shut when I was just a little girl,
told that my existence made others uncomfortable
and it was better to hide
than force myself on the world,
so I created my own little planet
out of pillows and a blanket
and began every morning
by adding a new stitch of my own.

LIAT SILVER

I fear for the day when I am an adult,
when I will lose the comfort and safety
of my silence,
when my thread will be forcibly cut
and I'll be thrown across that boundary
I was once too young to cross.
I fear for that day,
since it means I will be the one to sew someone else's
mouth shut
and teach them to find comfort in pain and silence.

As I sat there in the bath,
a million thoughts crossed my mind.
I couldn't help but think about the curve of my spine
as I hugged my knees to my chest,
thinking of times before that I'd stayed in this exact position
almost paralyzed by the water.
I've come to realize that the temperature of the water
dictates my mood.
I need the water hot
every few minutes adding more and more
scalding water till I feel that I may melt or fade away.
Years ago I used to sit in cold water,
I remember my teeth chattering and my skin stinging,
but I told myself that it was good for me
since it hurt less.
I remember all the times I've sat in this tub
big enough to fit me and my sister when we were so much younger,
and I held myself so that I occupied even less space than when
I was a child.
Memories are sparked from the strangest experiences.
I don't know why the lightheaded sensation
I feel as I sit in too-warm water brings me back
to the days that I try so hard to forget,

brings me back to the cold,
the stinging,
the blood slowly tinting the water,
to the scars that are unfortunately still a part of me.
At moments like this I feel powerless,
so maybe as a coping mechanism
I once again hold my knees to my chest
and pray that if I hold on tight enough
the glue that has held me together for so long
will not dissolve tonight.

They tell me I am small and should be happy about that,
yet I never feel happy when I trail behind others as we walk.
For every one of their steps
I feel as though I've taken a thousand.
They tell me boys will love me
since I am small and so adorable.
Then how come I feel so defenseless when a boy towers over me.
It doesn't feel cute when I'm living in constant fear of
ending up in the hands of someone stronger than me.
My mom tells me I am small
and cannot imagine me any other shape or size
but what if I cannot stay small forever,
will I no longer be the daughter she knows and loves?
Will I no longer be me?
My parents fear for my safety since I am so small.
They are afraid I may be carried away
with the wind one day.
They're petrified I'll end up in the pockets of a
stranger who took advantage of my size.
My parents fear for my safety
since I am so small,
yet I cannot grow any bigger
and have failed every attempt

to shrink further into myself.
My entire life I have felt so unbearably small,
almost as if I could slip through a crack in the window
and no one would notice I was gone.
My whole life I have been so small and still felt
as if I've taken too much space.
I guess size is an illusion.

WRITING FOR ALL THE WRONG REASONS

How much do you think a person can endure
before they physically break?
The question of course is rhetorical
since every person is different,
some can have all their bones break and walk away fine,
while others could drag paper against their skin
and shatter like glass.
This question used to keep me up at night,
leaving me to wonder if I was fortunate enough
to be made of stone,
crafted of marble,
or if I was made of glass
and the slightest shake could break me.
I now know that I am made of a material flimsier than glass.
I am the ribbon you place in typewriters,
I can only help when you are forcing the words onto me,
and with every push from your hands that I am at the mercy of
I lose a little bit of myself
but gain a mark from the metal you held against me.
I am easily replaceable.
Once my ink runs out,
and I have nothing left of me to lose,
those hands that haunt me at my every waking moment

reach out and remove me from my safe holding
and throw me away.
I will never be fortunate enough to break or fall apart,
I can only be marked and scarred
by actions that are not my own
until I have no room left to spare.

Saying Goodbye

WRITING FOR ALL THE WRONG REASONS

I wrote about everything,
all the loneliness,
the despair,
even the emptiness,
I accidentally took notes on my entire existence.
I wrote in place of feelings
all those years that I felt numb,
I wrote in fear of erasing myself,
the days that passed without me speaking a word,
the unknown safety in writing them instead;
I wrote instead of sharing my pain,
the years I spent destroying myself in silence.
I captured my world on these pages,
I told my story,
the story of a girl who was afraid of the real world,
I wrote about her growth,
both from child to adult
and from sick to strong.
I wrote about her humanity,
the world she wanted to create
a world where people like her could feel safe.
These words became a part of me,
aided in my recovery,

mended the broken parts of me,
and acted as the glue that held me together.
I have spent the past few years writing about everything,
documenting my experiences,
writing a biography of myself made of poetry—
"the poet's guide to living."

So now you have done it,
you have picked apart my brain
and seen the stories and the secrets
I have been keeping inside,
will you think any differently of me now?
Am I no longer the same daughter?
The same sister?
Am I now someone new?
I apologize if it was as hard
for you to read this as it was for me to write.
It's never been easy to open myself up
for rejection and proudly display
the words I spent years burying,
but I am stronger now than I was
when all of this began
and I hope you are stronger too
after reading my struggles.

www.ingramcontent.com/pod-product-compliance
Lightning Source LLC
Chambersburg PA
CBHW022108040426
42451CB00007B/176